A Prolapse of Mind

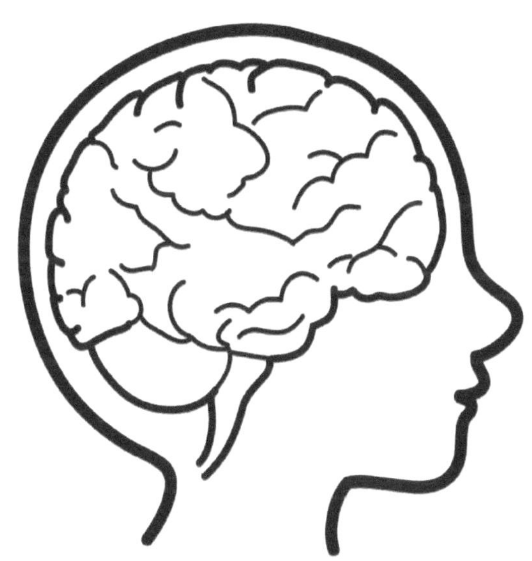

Jim Young

First Edition: 2021
Rs. 200/-

Cyberwit.net
HIG 45 Kaushambi Kunj, Kalindipuram
Allahabad - 211011 (U.P.) India
http://www.cyberwit.net
Tel: +(91) 9415091004 +(91) (532) 2552257
E-mail: info@cyberwit.net

Printed at Repro India Limited.

Contents

phoenix me not

a sub-atomic feather fell
from the phoenix that is rising
in the regresses of your mind
it tried to rise again   it really did
but downhill the wild horses cantered
trampling the embers in their snorting
that time be hoofed by no one
not even you - not even you
there
i've said it
how acrid is the feather's burning
the illusive anagram that is phoenix
in a mutual annihilation
the serpent bites its tail

who are the graffiti writers

who are the graffiti writers
down the unsavoury places
leaving bits of social psychology
artifice in your eyes
for they have stolen your thoughts
and sprayed them back in your face
tear gassed the mass hysteria
tearing past in a train
thoughts of nought in mid distance
but they shock you - oh yes
in their normality
'they' are accepted as being not all there
but where are they now the graffiti artists
fast asleep in your vacated beds
begs the thoughts of who has cuckolded
your inner thoughts seduced
your head turned missionary position
as the glass tunnels truncate past
your fingers grasp the metaphor
of the white knuckles in your fist
oh to write my bit of graffiti
and burn the bastards
wherever they i be

re: place

so easy to say
what we have taken away
but try as we might
it is not easy
even in the night
to replace
 re: place
somewhere else's problem
my innocence on a plinth
in the stocks of a pillory
lick the filigree of bronze
let the patina sting
so i may sing
tonight
tonight

at the beating of our capitulation

turning for help we found
the poem was merely a mirror
no more than no more
so we smashed it
licked at the silver sinews
and spoke in bloody tongues
corked in the swallowing
bloodshot eyes staring retort
we throttled their fisted throats
stamped the impression that we had won
but the words reassembled
mercurially re-globulating
the poem shivered at its newness
its fragility burnishing its finality
how the insane laughed and laughed
at this
at the beating of our capitulation

a

sepia
  grainy
 blurred
photo -
grapher
where are you now
dead i suppose
snapped
 it
   was
 not
in those days it was a science
i see my selfie
and chose
 sepia
   grainy
 blur
but science it is not
it is just another shot
in the dark
but i still recall your photograph
look
i have a snap of it here ...

talking on twitter

of all the deaths that could have been
of all the childhood risks to life unseen
to have survived is to say to you
i did not know but i do know now
that fate said meet me at the gate
and bring her close before too late
and we'll walk a while
and with a smile
forget regret
for
the museum has many wings
and many glass cases for many things
and dark corners that we turn and turn
we know them all and yet we learn
that ghosts have ghosts and we are are one
and the same goes on and on
in
the inestimable value of nothing in particular
that invaluable something
when isn't becomes is
lost

that field beside the road

it was just a road
that passed a field
along with a tree or two
it meant the world to you
on a summer day
when the grasses sway
as the flies do
what the flowers do
and you and me
sat quietly
in that field
beside the road

interlocutors

to be your very interlocutor
to lead them a merry dance
to claim before you came
this was my very name
for my name was interlocutor
and that was not by chance
                              so take
the happy from the happenstance
now here is your very chance
to take the art from artifice
and lead them a merry dance

and place before the world
what was not there before
for before it was there
you were there and more
to the point we were too
and we were so ...
how do you say it ...
interloculated

now gerra way with you

LOIME WE CALL IT

reading your poem
we tilt at the anger at anguish
the grit in the oyster is a tear
loime we call it
although such a word does not exist
we call it loime
for the pearls are puerile
too sweet and uniform strung
here is the prised clam
the cockle-less cockle shell
unhinged
filter feeding on your words
the sting of the tentacles
of so many thoughts redacted
below the tideline the wait is diurnal
again and again the tears of your grit
loime we call it
what do you call it
if anything
do you recall

 that i
that looks me in the eye
i do not know

you
i am talking to
you

me
i am nobody
don't change the subject

i know your game
oh yes
I know your game

"How time has ticked a heaven round the stars".

after the portrait
before the ink had dried
the sitter was gone

how did he know
the poet with his pile of words
what was hidden there

i gag in crying
for the child's night spun down
Swansea boys running

do you think we ought
to linger on his shadow
and kidnap a word

what stirs the damp wind
that the apple blossom snows
upon winter's death

times past
when the poet's pen is raised
be sure you listen

poet's hermitage
pilgrims looking for clues
are clueless

50 - always

a fingertip away from love
in the abstract that is life
behind the confusing canvas
in the abstract that is wife

she calls me her husband
i call her my wife
we've been together 50 years
that is nearly all my adult life

she sees in me what i cannot see
when all i see is wife
we both see our children
the reasons for all our life

the blossoms going over
for now it's that time of life
when she says i love you husband
and i say i love you wife

for now our days are numbered
under the long knife that cuts life
we wonder who'll get the last word in
goodbye husband or goodbye wife

the bird that forgot its song

the saddest thing i have ever heard
is about the rarest the rarest bird
that has forgotten how to sing its bong

how to sing its ~ dong

how to sing its ~ gong

how to sing its long

demise of all that the world meant to me
that things are not as they were meant to be
that the birds no longer sing to mate
i really do think that it is all too late

for a poet who has forgotten how to write

dreams

where is this world called dreams
is it where dreams are born
or is it where dreams go
to die

or to live the dream

because here there are only dreams
here mundane spells mundane
for dreams are always rudely awakened
slapped

oh where is this world called dreams

the night the moon broke

the night the moon broke
at full tide on a high tide
the lighthouse
     the lighthouse
flashing on all the little wavelets
but no moon after waiting
the obligatory

it's broke
  it's broke
i'm telling you the moon's broke
the moon's broke
and no one knows it
yet

Without the shadow of a doubt

Wouldn't it be interesting to live in a world of shadows?
Not the dramatic shadows of the movies, of the "Third Man"
sort,
but the shadows from a hair brush on a slanted sunbeam,
or from a fork in the candlelight of a dinner.
Of course you would also be a weird shadow,
but would your thoughts be the same?
Would real shadows be unreal and unreal shadows real?
What is the shape of a shadow of a doubt?
The angular shadows that move in the sun, hard
against a red wall or a dazzling white. They are dichotomous
within the thinking in the blinking of an eye. A light that flickers
sending
the shadows peeling. The stare renders them a negative positive
fluctuance. A retinal searing of slow time's resolution.
All shadow is night without lights. The obvious ambivalence
of a line drawn where no line is adumbrated but upon
the shifting borders of a light's fleeting presence.
A shadow cannot be scooped up and stored in a box;
or trapped in a jar. Can a light?
Without the shadow of a doubt I am sure doubtful it can? not?

yellow warning

false alarm -
it's the man with a pole
who listens down the hole
with a yellow jacket on
not the hole
the man
with the pole
he has not come to fill the hole
that is the goal for the man without a pole
who has not yet arrived to fill the hole
so a real alarm
that the hole will be a permanent feature
of worry when i see any man in a yellow jacket
with or without a pole
who looks down into my hole
there   see
i have taken possession of the hole
please send yellow jacket
ASAP

N THERE

to look at
in   THERE
[yes {in there} no]
the future in the darkness
in the mystery volleyed
between protagonists
the one surviving passion
signposted by curves of
sentience in scent intent
on irresistibleness
in lines aye
in the falling in up into into
pheromone_d automate _d
a strabismus towards a point
that is blurred in secrecy
adipose padded of genetic design
co-evolved with desire
sublimated as it is consummated
in a pull of such gravitational
collapse as to obliterate thought itself
in the mirage of sentience
for desire in satiation is desired
perpetrated engorged disgorged
ablated in the ultimate act of
procreation
      go on
deny it if you will into your misted mirror
but clear the fog and the corruption
of the silvering is red real enough

the amalgam is mixed
the race is on
the consummation is imminent
move on now
away back down
back off
your time at the front is over
count your heartbeats
refocus your eyes
and sleep the torpor
of forever
thereafter

COVID-19

how some went in and never came out
twenty twenty yet it's called C-19
a bit unwell what's all this fuss about

a tickly cough nothing at all to shout about
i'm fine and checking the twitter scene
how some went in and never came out

but i am fine and feel such a lazy lout
fussing over a slight temperature well i mean
a bit unwell what's all this fuss about

off my food a bit and can taste nought
can't even smell the cut grasses green
how some went in and never came out

a bit of a headache so please don't shout
that i should ask doctor to be seen
a bit unwell what's all this fuss about

time to go in to see what it's all about
a bit of oxygen before the ventilator screen
how some went in and never came out
a bit unwell what's all this fuss about

thin skin

          a float
with just (a) small weight
keeping me upright
in   choppy
      the   water
all the bait has been crabbed
bare hook (J) with
nothing to attract
even a small nod
to say   yes
he is was a poet
not one of the greats
   perhaps
with their reams of
tartan flies
no bait you see
   ~~ shallow water ~~
no small sleight of hand
no flick of the wrist lines
no
more like thick guy ropes
that hold contented down
when flight was called
clipped wings hopped
                              after them
looked at their soaring
   { { flying south } }
while he wintered
oh yes he wintered

wait

listening to the old songs
moving when we were
moving so slowly just to stand still
moving as slow as glass pours years
eyes shut as tight as breath allows
the third eye crying how could we
something something something
forgotten now what it was
other than the ache we had for it
it it it
drips as a net at a damp window
nets the cold night's ineptitude
looking for that chink of light
through those curtained days
around and around looking
for something we would not recognise
if we ever found it
and yet the music incanted that it
did exist somewhere this something
the others dancing knew
didn't they
and why if they did
didn't they say
didn't they tell me
no matter how the music spoke
the language was foreign even
as the beat beat it into me

wait
    wait
        wait

i nearly said

 looking for the reflection of self
the other half of the ticket for the ferry
to cross over after you
on the other side of me
the doppelgänger of a smile
in the mirror that brings death to life

i nearly said life to death

in Paris in black and white

who will share in black and white
a street light in Paris on a winter's night
cigarette glow in snow and smoke and mist
wet cobbled hills up slow Montmartre

and who will walk the talking walk
along the postered whispered boulevard
adverts tattered of gowns on boards
soaked in tears this city end of night

arming hearts once paired in dance
down hours lit of dimming light
down everything that dims the thought
that no thoughts may pertain

and all in black and white
at the very very end of night
cry stop do stay do not go
but gone is now the morrow that

has broken faith and dawned and crept away
on this time-startled dawn
and slept is never the ended word
at the end of a street
in Paris
in black and white

runes

and now the ruins have arrived
in lately eyes upon these times
torrid being the pandemic word
that best describe these times

we used to come as kids to the ruins
but there is no hope now for play it seems
for the memes in the fountain are rueing
over what best describe these times

for it is a bombers moon that climbs
silver under the boys flight feet
for no longer can we meet
to blast these blasted times

for even the ruins are ruined
where they were once pastimes
now they are in rusting derelict
mistrusting over time's deep mines

you can trust rust

rust is, well, sort of ...
menstrual;
in a, sort of, flow of time
sort of way.
a cleaning down
of yesterday's hopes
in readiness.
ah! rediness
always make a joke about it,
the blushing at ready time.
but seriously,
bits fall off and pile up and
over time the thing is nothing,
no more the thing we thought.
you cannot polish rust,
you have to bang it off
with the brutalism of decision.
start to build a wall around it,
lay the foundation bolts shining
build the phoenix's perch.

nothing is such a big word

it was a small case
not a valise
that's a posh word
no!
it was a small brown case
   shaped like a suitcase
with a handle that moved like a playground jerker
no it was not leather it was
                 ar tif ic ial
like every part of this bloody farce

the inventory
or should that be outventory
laugh - i nearly cried
the list as short as a full stop
   "patient's property"
impatient to be signed off
sent in a different direction

nothing personal
no!
what i mean is
there was nothing personal in there
just facecloth sort of things
i was carrying away nothing
he was now nothing
he was on a cold slab with his false teeth
soon to be cremated
returned to sender

i threw them in the bin
the nothings
dusting out the case i started to fill it
with memories
used my tears to shine it like real leather
i found that is was always half-full
stuffing it with everything everywhere
it was always half-full
 ::nothing::
is such a big word

(i'm off)

here
(throws them up in the air)
take the bloody lot
suit yourself
eat in plenty from the menu
or leave aside
here
(kicks them across the floor)
suit yourself
pick up the flower buds
or step on the bugs
here
(shouting and turning)
you lot i'm talking to the lot of you
you all have personal tastes
here is a trough for you
here
(dollops it in)
swill this around your mouth
swallow the sweet
puke up the poisoned words
more than enough to go around
here
i'm off
(snapping the pencils)
write your bloody own
i've dumped my dump
between these mountebank pages
caveat emptor
every jail a palace
every palace a jail

look - lest you ever forget

winter
it snows
we take photographs
blizzards of them
remembering
crumbs of comfort
budding clichés
spring will be
and soon enough
we'll take the photographs
remembering
the opening of the soil
the snoooooooze of summer
languid the lens
dazzling the days
in so many many ways
fades the photographic colour
sepia smiles autumn
falling over the mulch
of clichéd photographs
snowing of leaves
like the snow we photographed
blizzards of them
a photograph of a year book
placed inside the year book
for a photograph
look - lest you ever forget
the lens is the wheel
on the cycle of life

wobbling now and then
sometimes going arse over tit
into the shit
now that really is a photograph

My zinc bath

I bathed in a zinc bath in front of the fire
My Airsporter rifle could punch holes in a zinc bath
I grew spuds in a zinc bath
I kept frogs in a zinc bath
Seen them rusted through - eventually
Like a childhood enthral
Drummed on them with sticks
Small ones and large ones
Long ones and oval ones
Ones with a soap suds layer
Ones with a grit bottom
Ones with a scrubbing board and carbolic
Two handles to spill a dream
One handle to hang to dry
One day on another day
I will look back on the bath
And laugh

on that peak again

i'm reading keats and i am back again
at a desk hand polished and
scoured by compasses
indeed
signed deep with ink and slammed
shut on fingers to be tucked under
knees benched hard in concentration
on the words read loud and chalked
off sir's gown pacing and parsing the words
back and forth we recite
in the feeling
that it is our turn on that peak in darien
and i am at that very desk again
and we are reading keats again
and again and again

branched

calligraphied there in the snow
cliché black and twisted bent where
the wind has leant for far too long
upon the gaunt thought of waiting
upon the drifting
upon the blurring
of eyes closed in the twirling
one to the other's turning
silk like
trance like
beneath any understanding of the why
the branching sought the touching of fingertips
budding in the touching
in the turning one to another
touching as urgent as the wind presses the moment into being
into the consummation
the way the tree relaxes when the snow drops
as we turn prone to the tracing of the footsteps
that merged under the snow's dawning
and now
asleep in the time that has had its time
knowing
not what that was
other than that it was now
that the black branches remembered the spring
the tight buds pulsed almost imperceptibly
in everything everywhere there was a pregnancy
in the untwirling of spliced time

and then there are the windows

the ones with steamy tears
freezing into art
or the bottle-bottom ones
squirming at the thought
of the leaves trying to get in
or out depending on the thought
nailed in screeching down the panesss

the rolling races to the bottom
besmirch spoiled by the finger
pointing out the lights on the horizon
or the black ones reflecting
if outside is inside or vice versa
is in the eyes

the stark trees of winter
corkscrewed by the rain
or the deciduous of summer
dancing green

the cracked ones loved
or neglected lost to thoughts
of who they were the dwellers
and can we see in on them
even now
after the spiders have laced the shroud

the picture windows
the matrix panes with just one

or two shot out by time's arrow
defenestrated - isn't that what they say
of the rusty

the boundary condition
the stopping of flattened palms
leaving minds to wander alone
over the edges that draw blood
in the dust of a stopped thought

close them now
  please
i need to sleep
and there is this draught
draw the curtains
lock the windows of inside out

sorry

it's like one of them horror films
where the walls with spikes move in
unstoppable in their promiscuity

a pandemic of global issues
incurable in their extinctions
no hope at all of steering through
before the walls impale

the pallor of youth never to brogue
in the veined cheeks of age
or ring grey the eyes of looking

that sinking feeling on the marsh
with overpopulation floating upon the threat
of mass the extinction of any hope
orphaned unnurtured terminal

the velocity of our demise
repeated over and over
it is true   but
the end
seems so final - does it not

finally we see how blind we were
blind to the abyss
over the annihilation of hope

and that is the very end of it
unfortunately the anodyne word
for there will be no one left to hear
i am really sorry

me I said

for a minute there I had no idea where I was
where for a minute I had no idea I was there
there there I said to myself
when someone answered
who are you
where did the voice come from
I asked
where does the voice come from
it asked

me I said

nasty is a word

words can be nasty
in the wrong company
they can walk you through the garden
up the growing lane into a dark alley
and knife you in the guts
wipe the knife and knife you
in the guts
then leave you to
exsanguinate
now there's a bleeding word for you

on the dunes of the year

on the dunes of the year
the fences slip
the sand drifts
what we did is blown everywhere
for all to see
what we did
has exposed the long roots of
the marram grass that ends
on what everyone else
may think
and we never know do we
what they are thinking i mean
how their tides flow
how the long light falls
all we know is that everything changes
the fences are secondary pickets
for at the end
our days are numbered thus

a bunch of kids

the future is this bunch of kids,
* what they do not know , , , , ,
now,
* is that one day they will not know , , , , ,
how,
* time flew away the way it did, , , , , ,
* the way it did   the way it did, , , , ,
and stole their innocence,
* and bestowed it on a bunch of kids, , , , , ,

a chapel in dereliction

the chapel in need is now green stoned
down derelict black on dusty pews
fallen like snow on crunched slate prayers
long dead bereft the once good news

the coming ages dumb long gone
and god-only-knows the where's
and the why-fors of iced bones turned
in graves where once lights shone

or shimmied off the felled bible stands
page numbers splayed and crooked lined
dampening forever all causes so inclined
where bare stark wires in witness strands

or doors so unhinged as to sarcophagate
that which was once heaven's narrow gate
thrown wide now to the congealing wind
enveiled in moss on walls ingrained

in the devil's footsteps how we hate
the run of time's thoughts as if preordained
kiltered high where rusting time berates
our anguished cries in silence screamed
why can we not awaken from this dream
this nightmare that in timeless time
why why has all returned to grime

chapel so silent in an emptiness now
with ne'er a thought with ne'er a prayer
however long your look before you turn to ask how
answer says there is nothing here there is nothing there
that will dare reply to you
other than to commiserate
there there my lonely child
be still in this your grieving
mercy can and will be mild
if you go on believing
that dereliction can be
and this a new beginning

A lesson in the school of hard knocks,

* Life (IS) unfair, , , , , ,

* It shouldn't be, , , , , ,
* It needn't be, , , , , ,

* But is (IS,), , , , ,

* If we ever 'sort it' then, , , , , ,
* Hey up, !, , , , ,
* Along comes death, , , , , ,

after watching a BBC documentary

now
there is mercury in the whales of the faroes
and the birds they are dying in kind
for the tunnels from the past to the future
may be turning the tides of the mind
    then they come all the sentimentalists
with their databanks of absolute validity
when decrying of 'this 'barbaric slaughter'
are they talking to you or to me?
    for the blood you see staining the harbour
is arraigned in the mete of every man's quota
where the eating of whale meat and blubber
aughta keep us strong upon a stormy sea
    and the ropes and the boats and the daring
bring home the winged harvest of the time lines you see
that are etched on their wind-red faces preparing
to risk everything thing for you and for me
    and for our kids say the beautiful mothers
in their coloured houses and national dress
for on that day there is never any mourning
just our stress on the rare life of these isles
and one imagines what the smiles of the elders will be
when they hear the faroese kids fondly say
that this is a must place for me

and what if

and what if the sun does not rise
as it always has but now does not
the cat cannot read but looks at a book
doesn't know the start from the finish
but will sit on the book and think of washing
it always does and always will
but what if the sun does not rise
who will feed my cat
i ask you that but you have no bright ideas
no eureka bulbs come on
no dawn of thought
bugger! bugger! bugger!

autumn

where the seeds are blowing to the falling still
and sunlight spiders the pine cones fill
upon the limestone in a lichen sun
all that salts a coastal walk begun

step the fungi lightly on october's fields
where inquisitiveness wrapped in hushedness kneels
and dry grasses to the thistle rosette yields
the joy at the fullness that autumn feels

long-beamed the cooling setting sun
a crimson lancet across the calmest bay
warm rocks lament unrequited fun
as with tears in our eyes we swim away

hushed shadowed long and homeward bound
what was lost has now at last been found
and down all winters frozen paths
we will think of spring around glowing hearths

bury me with a book

bury me with a book
deep within a dingle nook
then whisper to the breeze
do not defame or even
whisper his name
save what the pages
in all of their sadness rages
shaking the tears from the trees
to lay upon a silver brook
to hook his seven seas

call me rough life

call me rough life
why do you not call me to play the fool
the arrogant roughneck drinking fool
that wrote for her - you know -
those lurid nights of windowed cities
and bars and wet streets and brawls in
in stairwells of brevity kisses
and traffic hisses away down town
and frowns and downs and downs
to wet knee wet with tears raining down with
your mascara and bruised love if
love it be for me and my philandering
why don't you rough me up and
leave me with enough smoke-stained angst
to write the brutal lines that all the great
do-no-good poets clawed
upon the page's confessions of regret
and fabled acerbic pounding of
relationships gone on far far too long past
their ability to even breathe an emotion

why this easy ambiance this ease of life
that pours not cider vinegar but maple syrup
that has not one word to cut the days of
blank pages and no looks that could kill
in red ink the slammed book of poems
dedicated in hatred to all whose meritocracy
i defied to entertain just my egotistical nonchalance

now that i bare write nothing nothing at all for
having not died in that life i lay down nothing

is it too late these aged years to ride
the bronco stallion of desire unbridled
and fly at last to the wild side of life
rattling penniless unrepentant galavanting
nailing dirty words smearing fetid words
bleeding grimy words spitting oathy words
leaving no stone of life unturned before
the days run down

is it too late
am i run to time run done
it is over mun
it is isn't it
and was it not i
who left it
all undone

f*alright 451,

when all have stockpiled panic,
* and the shelves are fully empty, , , , , ,
* all we'll have is empty in plenty , , , , ,
then when altruism dies,
* society follows , , , , ,
and ignores our cries.

* i'm f*alright 451, , , , , , ,

fluke?

what fluke
has loaned me this mind
that has infinite capacity (perhaps)
to think
before it is returned
to the infinite empty shelves
stretching empathy
in the library of nothing
that by definition is outside
of infinity (perhaps)
is it a fluke?

for in denial never truth were told

so strange this vicissitude to behold,
that these times now are falling overdue;
for in denial never truth were told.

when idiots rule the streets be bold,
and say 'no! not now' to these fevered few;
so strange this vicissitude to behold.

dying alone, no comfort hand to hold,
just the distant digital image of you;
for in denial never truth were told.

around this fear we must remould
a life stronger fairer resurgent new;
so strange this vicissitude to behold.

fiscal change can now be social gold,
revolution in these fraught times accrue.
so strange this vicissitude to behold,
for in denial never truth were told.

giving it the works

that pipe - hot to touch
that grumbling - in the guts
of the machine - that is
the works - the real works
where - the furnace smelts
the metals - the sintered gasses
cough eyed - the watering
of the men - the knowing that
the time for that - goes just there
always just there - and there
and there - is deep soiling
of the innards - from the in
to the out flowing - the flowering
of dirt into - well - into more dirt but
there is the shinning - the product
of all men's toils - smiling or grimacing
the teeth bite - the air does not move
it never moves - men go around it
around the hot pipes - the flow internal
eternal - the closeness of the distance
between here - and there
the smelting - of the days
the moulding - of the metal
the hopscotch men - dancing to the tune
of industry - cooling in the towers
of night shifts - blue lights
long walks - down burma road
out beyond knowing - that now you know
how the works - works it out
for you

hearth and tired

when the fire blew down on
the night of wind and rain
when the cat was deep and
all were chaired to the hearth
of unsaid family lines
the raising of hearts in times
that were as dark as the night sky
before the stars and the snowy moon
shining as the fender brass and the
poker glowing red as hell
those songs hanging forever on
sleepy eyelids and weary bones
in the downing days of heavy time
cadillac was as strange a meme
as winsome as the movie toffees
and the longing for the other side
of any walled hillside
or the veneered panelled walls
behind which the cockroaches slept
until the fire died and we were abed
and then they came over the coal-grit
to eat the crumbs of the crumbs
that our meagre dinners had left ledgered
here in this corner of a neglected village
in wales
a people tipped under slag and
toil so numbing that the sinews of life
crystallised in grime and death that never died
in relief of times best forgotten now

for when you think of it
we cried enough dryness
to last a lifetime

i'm building a haiku hermitage

i'm building a haiku hermitage
a haiku hermitage for one
when all the bad news rages
i'll sit there in the sun

and when the war is over
whether lost or won
i'll write another poem
to set beside this one

and then I'll look across the valley
to the sunrise in the west
and chant myself to sleep
home   home   home
is best

I fear for the morning

The wood pigeon asks Buddha if is there any food.
The Buddha stays silent in the eyes-closed snow.

The pigeon stalks off leaving little footprints.

They are slowly disappearing.

It is getting darker.

A last dunnock flits away.

No stars tonight
I fear for the morning.

in a dream's dream

in my dream
a dreaming poet
dreams of me

and she writes

he was dreaming
of me

in my dream

in deceasing december

the day darkens, rain is coming, they say
it is the lunatic asylum season,
these long dark days of december.
through the big window the day darkens,
reflections of table lamps pop up,
the pale blue sky pales blue to darken
a promise of rain upon a book's last leaves
rattling in the wind's turn over;
and there i am reflecting upon my reflection,
fathering further the past's surmise that
begs the curtains be drawn on the black thoughts;
for inside me the brightest of past decembers
remembers the comic's antics and the smiles
that would never end - even in these dark times
the drapes sleep me a dream upon a big sigh.

invisible ink

the well of tears that never empties
running between the lines
of no man's land
fur on the barbed wire
around the craters
tiny footprints
picking poppies
for mum

it is a matter of style

the tough words take no prisoners,
set no smoothed path,
hurl rocks at your head
ducking -
licking the grazed shins,
stumbling over realisations,
uncomfortable the shards in your shoes.

oh yes, the simple words can bring
the story to the sting,
can knife the guts up a sunlit lane;
but it's the tough words from the seams
deep in mind's mine, where the
pressure lodestones are, that
tole the indelible.

why can't the words soften?
become more gently feminine,
lead the child around the cataract?
why do they always raft the white waters,
spitting the urgency of the hindmost?

why the cynic?
why the chitin carapace?
the urgency of uprighting the beetle
onto the legs of the thematic
iridescence of the kingfisher
or the languidity of the auora.

the old leopard cannot change its spots,
the prey half recognises the leopard,
the slowness caresses the anticipation
that what is caught is small prey:
it is the hunting down,
the bringing down after the chase
that legs the arterial blood,
that satiates the telling.

on this fulcrum of indecision
it is i, the poet, who seeks guidance;
the wisdom of solomon,
the telling of the way.
am i lost? or is the destination?
and how will i ever know?

it's always been this way

on the last snow sunbeam long in down
the yellow moon rises ever so slowly
under the halo of a blue frost see its crown
slips ever so slightly in a kilter skew only
in this late of day does one's mind then drift
along cooling thoughts of thoughts turned home
and lift foot step after foot step lift
does approach distance itself to roam
to days where the days were nights
and mornings were mornings self-contained
when we were young enough to set world to rights
to never countenance that what remained
of life's mysteries were barely laid
than a snow of thoughts blown adrift
never to consider the price we paid
to reach the ferry's route of thrift
all stranded again on another shore
we panic about for the way to go
for youth's bank now is over drawn
and sallow is the fat of muscle brawn
for the moon is gone
the sun not dawned
all is lost in a
life forlorn

me see?

when you point at yourself where is it you are?

your knee - absurd
your shoulder -absurd
your head - might be - but don't feel like
right
you tap your sternum - closer
getting warmer
ah! - your heart - right?
well no - more in the centre
near the top of your sternum
close your eyes - sink through it
behind it (you / me) - come back! - wait for me!
oscillate through it - closer
does it move - slightly - like an unborn child's heartbeat?
maybe, maybe
look in the mirror - point at me / you
pointing at me / you
doesn't help a lot - does it?
hey you! - what me?
now, who replied - suddenly
being you - point to that spot
that momentarily is you
before it shamelessly diffuses
confuses you
but
why should you confuse you?
what is the point in hiding
the locus of you from you?

maybe it / you do not exist
in a - 'here i am' - sort of way
ever thought if that?
hey you! i'm talking to you
come back here - - -
now!

mum - it's late

fish scales, dark and light, silvering
the scour on the marbling of time;
thoughts from before my mother became
my late mother, and the long years
when the remembering was blank;
but now, peppered, a mixture of good and bad,
of light and dark, of smiles and tears,
that were spilled and were mopped up.

for now, all one can say is sorry,
more to one's self than to any diviner
of inner thoughts who might twig
that "mum - it's late" is not an admonishment
but an apology.

pocket me a field

pocket me a field, with frost in a corner,
mole hills along one side
of day's second quarter;
and here bid me abide
with days in my eyes and
the joys of winter, cold in surmise;
and i will surprise a cock pheasant
in rasp and in running,
the leaves all a flitter,
so very pleasant with frost all a glitter:
then turn me around and around
from the castle to the sea,
from the rivers to the sky
and then ask this of me,
was there ever such a day
as this set before thee?
go on, ask me again,
was there ever such a day
as this set before thee?

post-mortem

on the scent of a promised flower
of a summer we may yet live to see
in the depth of a meadow's bower
may you lay down low against me

and embrace the moment foretold
when to foretell was a difficult taste
to bake in an oven stone cold
a virus that was spreading in haste

and in this downing of days
down all of the reasoning of ways
lay no hope at the feet
than a bedraggled shroud sheet

that we will greet hand in hand
at the boundary of the boundary
of a promise promised land
social distanced deemed never to meet

for enough was never said
that they (it's always they)
would understand the way
that the virus is caught and is spread

far and wide and woe betide
the oxygen of yesterday
will run out today
and force the old songs that we deride

tip all the faith of youth
over the precipice
of a perception
that such an island uncouth

in a bravado of youth
is not an interesting notation
except to the bloody fuddy duddies
that are not a worthy foundation

for tomorrow is a new world
and what was culled was not
anything essential but
at best irreverential

and to beholden as 'them olden of days'
at the 2020 - 2021 boundary
when the virus was retooled
as a reaper of the unwary fool

the corollary of yesterday
being the repentance of today
the corollary of today being
that which is now lost

never to be found

remember
                        never
is a word oft repeated
but rarely understood

remembering the ephemeral childhoods of summer

what words have ploughed the furrowed sky
what eyes have widened with the why oh why
did i not see the end was nigh
did i not feel a cold damp sigh

that warm suns slipped away the days began
down all the lanes of childhood shrieking ran
bird nested egg shelled the colours shine
for every summer that said that it was mine

forever mine and never so to end
forever blue and warm and so my friend
i gave my heart away that summer's day
to fishing the running trout stream ere i die

of chasing the chasing of the cuckoo
of the cuckoo again across the way
the copses in the reed beds seem to say
that they cannot get me in this marshy goo

and do you know how the skylark flies
so high that the sky is all there is
the blue so blue that eyes surmise
that there is no end to its song of days

spent hovering across the moorland
purple pollened and lizard ran from
the bravado fire at the children's hand
in the land of the chasing man

in the land of rivers run
the land of the fox and hare
of beetles grubbed in fun and
here and there and now and then

there is always tomorrow
when the bloodied knees have dried
and the i didn't i didn't cried
and all that that implied

when the moon sheets tight
wrapped a candle's corner
sliding to sleep goodnight
at memory's border

until the bickering of the morning birds
bids fly on heels across the glory fields
where transience in infinite seems in order
a smile in memory of the squirrel hoarder
and then summer to autumn finally yields
and ephemeral says it's long goodbye
as childhood's shortening summers fly